Comfort & Joy book one: forgiveness

Marie McGaha

COMFORT & JOY:
Forgiveness

Marie McGaha

ALL RIGHTS RESERVED

Dancing With Bear Publishing is a registered trademark
Copyright Marie McGaha ©2015
ISBN 13: 978-0615627717
ISBN 10: 0615627717
for Elizabeth

DWB   PUBLISHING
www.dancingwithbearpublishing.com

Foreword

There are so many times in life when we feel completely alone, or so lonely we could die. We have no one to turn to and no one who would understand where we've been, or what we're feeling. We think we are being swallowed up by our circumstances and there is nowhere to turn.

I know because I've been there. I've used drugs and alcohol to forget, to ease the pain, to help me through each day, when what I really wanted was to take my own life and felt that I even failed at that task.

I was sexually abused as a child by two uncles. My parents were partiers and heavy-handed with the discipline. I ran away from home on many occasions from about age thirteen to when I left for good at age fifteen. I hitchhiked across the country, went from one place to another and one man to another, until at age sixteen, I found myself pregnant. My grandmother was a minister and had taken me to church all my life during the summers I spent with her. I knew who God was.

I knew Jesus had died for my sins, but I never could quite hold on to that thread for very long, except during times of deep trouble. I was a "rescue me Jesus" Christian, which meant I only depended on Him when I couldn't help myself. As soon as life straightened out a little bit, I was on my own again, and God was a distant memory.

My life went on like that through drugs, alcohol, partying, men, and the births of more children. I didn't know how to be a parent. I didn't know how to discipline my children because the only discipline I knew was beatings.

I remember when I was young, and after being whipped by my dad, he would cuddle me and say, "Daddy hates to spank you, but I do it because I love you."

In my mind, I always related love to being beaten, so no wonder I always sought out men who abused me. I had nothing to base a good, strong, loving relationship on. Other than my grandmother, there was no functional parental relationship and that left a huge void within me. So, I treated my children the same way I had been treated, and they paid the price for my inability to function as a loving mother should.

The thing I have discovered is that the one constant in my life is that I had a praying grandmother, and even though she died when I was twenty-three, God didn't forget her prayers. (Proverbs 15:29) *"The Lord is far from the wicked, but He hears the prayer of the righteous."* Although Grandma never got to see me saved while she was on earth, she knows God didn't forget her prayers, and I'm sure she knows I am now a child of God.

God does not change (Malachi 3:6). We change, our feelings change, our desires change, our direction changes but God does not change. Jesus Christ is the same yesterday, today and forever (Hebrews 13:8). And for that, I am forever grateful because of the Lord's steadfastness, my life changed. My changing persona didn't faze God one bit because He knew the plan He had for me before I was formed in the womb. (Jeremiah 29:11)

When I was seven years old, I saw the Lord come down a stairway into the bedroom where I slept at my grandmother's house. The bed had an iron frame, a mattress I sank into, and hand-made quilts that seemed to weigh fifty pounds. One morning I woke up to the usual sounds of my grandmother fixing breakfast for my grandfather, but it was so cold in the room, I didn't want to get out of bed.

Suddenly, the ceiling seemed to open, a great, bright cloud filled the room and a stair case slid down through the clouds into the room. Then, a Being walked down the staircase, wearing leather sandals, and I could see the hem of His garment, but He was so tall, I couldn't see any more than that. Somehow, I knew it was Jesus, and He wanted me to serve Him and see many souls led to Him. Then everything went back up into the ceiling and I jumped out of bed and ran into the kitchen.

I told my grandmother what happened, and she told me how special I was to have a 'visitation.' She also said she knew when I was born that I would serve God. I'm sure that was something she wished for all her grandchildren but at the time, I believed it was only for me. The next Sunday I accepted the Lord as my Savior. Since then, the devil has been trying to kill me.

~ * ~

As long as the devil can keep us looking *away* from God, we are looking at him instead. As long as we are worried about our lives, our jobs, or we are poor, distraught, lonely, high, depressed, drinking, or whatever else Satan can throw in our path, we are not paying attention to God. And that is exactly what he wants.

But the more we put our life, and life's

problems, into God's hands, the bigger targets we become. Although, when we stay under the wings of the Lord (Psalm 91:4), we will always be protected, no matter what the devil throws at us.

In this first book of Comfort & Joy, I am addressing forgiveness. This theme is a constant throughout the Bible, nevertheless, it is also the most difficult concept for us to grasp.

I pray that once you read this book, you will come away with a new perspective, a new outlook on the things that have weighed you down, and it will allow you to shed the unforgiveness, pain, anger, and all the other feelings that have kept you from being the person God wants you to be.

~ One ~

Forgiving those who have hurt us can be one of the most difficult things we ever have to do. In fact, it's so difficult that there is a popular saying, "I may forgive but I will never forget." I've even heard this come from

Christians, but nothing can be farther from the teachings of Christ.

1 John 1:9 tells us that, *"He forgives us and cleanses us from all unrighteousness."* Not only are we forgiven for our sins, but they are no longer remembered by God. He takes our sins, throws them into a Hefty Bag, and then tosses it into a big dump that only God has the directions to.

God is not a god who reminds us of our faults of yesterday but of our abilities through Him for all our tomorrows. God wants us to shine, to minister to others, to represent His Son, Jesus, wherever we go, and to win souls to the Kingdom of Heaven.

One of the biggest things we will have to do to accomplish this is to forgive and for-get our own past. Yes, I said to *forget* the past, not just forgive the past but forget it ever existed. That includes not only forgiving others but one's self, which is a difficult task, I know.

I am one of those people who bear the weight of the world on their shoulders. I think that I am responsible for everything everyone else does, and if I had just said or done one thing differently, the entire outcome of everyone else's lives would be different. I ride on waves of guilt that
seem to well up within me from nowhere at all. I allow the consequences of other people's actions to land on me and make me feel as if I am responsible for what they have done.

What I had to come to terms with is *I am not God*. Imagine that—I am just one of several billion people who occupy earth and take up oxygen, living a very ordinary life. I cannot make anyone do or say anything they don't want to and beating myself up over what other's do only drives me farther from the love and grace of God.

I have laid in bed crying in anguish over my ex-husband who died. I was so distraught over his passing and convinced that I could have done or said something to
someone, somewhere, that would have pre-

vented his death. I loved this man for more than half my life and his passing felt as if it would destroy me. It was just one more thing the devil had in his arsenal against me, and he used it well.

The truth is, the devil is out to kill, steal, and destroy (John 10:10) your life on earth, and ultimately, your soul. He doesn't want you to live happily with God's blessings, no, he wants you to be miserable and unhappy, and he wants your soul in Hell with him. There is a saying among Christians, "We know how the story ends and the devil loses." Yes, he loses but, in the meantime, he is active in this world to make sure he takes down as many of us as he can in the time he has left.

So, how does the devil work? Unbelief is his greatest ally. For those who don't believe in God, the devil doesn't really have to worry about them. He knows they have what they want—money, drugs, fame, or whatever it is—and that is their reward. But for those of us who believe in God, who believe Jesus is the Savior of the world, we can expect the devil to do his best to destroy our lives. The devil is a coward, he never just confronts us directly, no, he likes to use those things that make us most vulnerable. The biggest of those is our past. Don't we all let our past get to us? Don't we obsess on all the things we have done wrong in our lives? And don't we dwell on the things others have done to us? These are the devil's weapons. He knows where to jab, punch, and kick. He knows how to use our guilt and unhappiness against us.

The Bible describes the devil as *"...your great adversary, the devil... prowls around like a roaring lion, looking for someone to devour."* (1 Peter 5:8) But verse nine says, *"Stand firm against him, and be strong in your faith..."*

So, the only way to defeat the devil is to be strong in our faith in Jesus Christ and the Word of God, the Bible.

I know sometimes that is so difficult, especially if you are new to Christianity and are just learning the Bible. When we are brand new, baby Christians, we still have our old non-Christian baggage that we drag around behind us. We haven't figured out yet how to let it go, or what to do with it. And the devil knows this.

What is inside your bag? Were you hurt as a child? Abused physically, sexually, emotionally? Have you been raped, lived with an abusive partner, or been a drug addict? Were you a prostitute? Do you have a sexually transmitted disease there is no cure for? Were you a criminal, served time in prison? Or perhaps nothing in your life has ever worked out for you, and everything you have tried to do has come to nothing?

No matter what is in your bag, God can rid you of it, but the first step is allowing God to have full control of your life. And to allow God to do that means to forgive yourself and those who have harmed you.

Are you cringing inside at the thought of forgiving the person who beat you, molested you, raped you, robbed you, or otherwise hurt you? That's all right. God is big enough that He can handle whatever you are hiding inside of yourself, praying no one ever sees.

God is the One who created the Heavens and the Earth, man, and woman, all the animals, oceans and everything that lives there. He is the One who loved us so much, He sent His only begotten Son to die a horrible death on the cross so that you and I will not have to pay for our own sins. Jesus Christ became sin for us, and all we must do is ask Him to forgive us and live our lives for Him, according to His word.

Seem too good to be true? Have you

heard someone tell you how they loved you,
would care for you, and never let harm come
to you, for them to only turn on you? Has the
very one who should protect you been the one
to hurt you and let you down? Are you afraid to
trust, to love, to believe there can possibly be
someone who will never leave or forsake you?
Is forgiveness a concept so foreign that you
can't even think about it?

We have all felt that way at one time or
another. Not one of us has skated through life
without anger, hurt feelings, or having someone we know take advantage of us. That is
human nature, a sinful nature that we are all
born with. But it doesn't have to be that way,
and through faith in Jesus Christ, it won't continue to be that way.

Jesus Christ is the perfect Lamb of God,
sacrificed for our sinful nature, and we can believe and trust in Him. We can trust in the Lord
God and turn our lives, love, and trust over to
Him, knowing He will handle us with loving
care.

~ Two ~

None of us had perfect parents. I know some people who have had parents that came close, but we are all human and fallible. God the Father is not fallible. He is the perfect father and He wants us to come to Him as children. He wants a father/child relationship with each of us.

But how do we let ourselves believe that kind of relationship can exist? How do we let go of everything that hinders our acceptance of all that God has to offer? How do we trust in God, who we can't see, when we can't even trust in someone we can see?

Hebrews 12:1 tells us to *"...strip off every weight that slows us down, especially the sin that so easily trips us up..."* That is how we run the race to finish as winners.

So, what are those sins that so easily trip us up? I believe they begin with one thing—unforgiveness.

Unforgiveness is a demon just waiting to pounce on us at any given moment. It hammers away inside of us like a chisel chipping away at a giant rock, and makes us feel insecure, angry, bitter, and resentful. It robs us of our joy, happiness, and interferes with our lives and relationships. Unforgiveness keeps us from accomplishing the plans God has for us, and ultimately, keeps us from being forgiven.

Seems rather harsh, doesn't it? Matthew 6:14 & 15 says, *"If you forgive those who sin against you, your heavenly Father will forgive you. But if you refuse to forgive others, your Father will not forgive your sins."*

Why would God say that? What does forgiving others have to do with our own forgiveness from God? For one thing, we are *not* God, so who are we to not forgive others when He has forgiven us? Secondly, whatever God gives us, we are to pass on to others.

He gives us love, compassion, hope, joy, and forgiveness, and we are to give that to everyone we know and those we meet. But when there is unforgiveness in our hearts, we cannot pass on love to someone we despise. When we cannot pass on those things from God, we lose the joy God intends for us as Christians.

I can hear someone saying, "There is no way I can forgive _____ for what they did to me!" I was that way, too. I had a list of who I would not, and could not, possibly forgive but what I learned was that not forgiving them didn't have one iota of effect on them, but it sure did on me. I was angry, hurt, resentful, and I took it out on myself and everyone around me.

The unforgiveness inside of me affected every area of my life and caused me to act out in a variety of unhealthy ways. I drank, I used drugs, and I slept with men, and sometimes, I didn't even know their names. I was a wreck and didn't even know it.

~ * ~

My Story: I had been molested from about age three to age eleven by my dad's oldest brother. I remember him taking me to his basement workshop and putting me on the worktable, removing my pants, and telling me, "Once the head is in, it won't hurt anymore." I was so young that of course, what he wanted to do just wasn't going to happen. When I cried, he told me to shut up, and finally, when I couldn't stop crying, he would let me go. He threatened that if I told my parents, he would tell my dad I was lying, and I knew what my dad would do if I lied.

Of course, I knew. My parents were strict, and I knew they would believe an adult over me. I was just a kid, so I didn't tell, and I suffered his abuse every time we went to visit. When we finally moved away was the greatest day of my life.

However, when I was about seven, my mom's youngest brother came home from Vietnam and live with us. He began molesting me too, but instead of doing to me what my dad's brother did, my mom's brother only wanted
me to touch him. In my young, messed up mind, I thought it was so much better than what my dad's brother did, that it must not be as wrong.

But when I was about eleven I did tell on my dad's brother. My mother's words were, "You must have liked it or you wouldn't have waited this long to tell."

So here I was, so very young, so hurt physically and mentally, and devastated by what my mother said. I do remember her wanting my dad to tell the police, but he said no one would believe a kid over an adult. That was the way things worked then. And the kids that weren't believed suffered for it.

When puberty set in, I went crazy. Literally, out-of-my-mind crazy. I began acting out, running away from home, sneaking around, drinking, smoking cigarettes, smoking weed, and sleeping around. When I finally left home for good, I hitchhiked all over the country, sleeping with truck drivers, partying with people who were five or ten years older, and only as an adult did I see how lucky I was not to have been killed, or worse.

After I had several children, all from different men, did I see how self-destructive I was. The problem was, I didn't know what to do about it. I didn't know how to stop, and I think now about my poor children, especially the older two, having to live through my craziness. I was a horrible mother but how could I be anything else? I had no idea what I was doing, much less how to parent.

I began using more drugs, methamphetamine, cocaine, LSD, and whatever else might be handy. But the meth was my drug of choice. So, on top of crazy, I was messed up on drugs most of the time, which was really the only thing that kept me from feeling like I was crazy. It wasn't until after I met my late husband, J. "Bear" Marler, that I realized just how far out of my mind I had gone.

I got off the drugs and cleaned up my life but there was still something wrong with me. I had no idea what it was because in my family, no one had "issues", there was no going to therapy, and no psych meds to keep one sane. In fact, the only thing I remember my father saying was that my mother was crazy, I was crazy, and anyone who didn't think the way he did was crazy. I never took the term seriously because it had no real meaning. But I was crazy in the very literal sense of the word. I'd been beaten about the head numerous times, knocked unconscious, and later on in my life, I learned I had a few neurons that weren't firing correctly, not to mention the damage inflicted by both the beatings and the drugs. I needed help that I didn't get until much later.

In 1994, Bear and I both accepted Christ as our Savior, studied to become licensed ministers and then were ordained. We served God and traveled across the country preaching at churches, storefront ministries, and to bikers, hookers, pimps, drug addicts, convicts, and all those people that others kind of ignored. We had a wonderful ministry, a wonderful marriage and things were great... or so it seemed. I wasn't great. I was bitter, confused, angry, resentful, and I lashed out at those closest, which meant Bear and the kids took the brunt of my rage. I didn't know why I did the things I did. I couldn't explain it and I couldn't live with it. I spent hours on the floor of the bathroom crying and praying because I knew the only One who could answer was God. The answers didn't come immediately but they did come.

One Christmas, Bear and I invited anyone in our church who would not have family to our home, and we had quite a house full. One of those people was a lady who had only been in our church, along with her husband, a short while. She was blind, had white hair, dressed in square dance dresses, and said her name was Sister Pianoheart.

While we were sitting and talking, she and I began talking about losing our children. Bear and I had a daughter (from Bear's first wife), Cassandra, who died at age sixteen. Sister Pianoheart told me she had a son who had been killed at age seventeen. I told her how sorry I was but her answer to me was, "His death served a purpose for God, and I think you have unforgiveness in your heart that is holding you back."

I looked at her and began to tear up. I knew she was right. I not only had unforgiveness, I had sheer unadulterated hatred in my heart for my dad's brother, my mom's brother, for every man who had used me as a punching bag, had abused me or my children, and I felt as if they owed me something.

I felt as if somewhere there had to be a big chalkboard with my name on it followed by these horrid people who had hurt me physically, mentally, and emotionally. I wanted them to apologize, to grovel at my feet and beg my forgiveness. I didn't want to just give them forgiveness—they didn't have the right to that.

Not only that, my dad's brother had died in 1988 after a long battle with lung cancer. A battle I was sorry to see him lose because I wanted him to continue to suffer and to be in pain. Each time they cut away another piece of his lung, I wanted him to remember it was his payment for all the hurt he had caused the little girl inside of me who still cried at night for the innocence she lost.

My dad came to my house on his way to the funeral for his brother and I told him I was sorry he lost a brother,
but as for me, I hoped his brother rotted in Hell. I wanted to go to the cemetery and dance on his brother's grave in a red dress and high heels. As far as I was concerned, Hell was too good for him. I wished I could see his suffering, flames licking at his feet, him scream-

ing from the unbearable pain, and his thirst unquenchable.

But that Christmas day, some six years later, would change my life and outlook forever. Sister Pianoheart told me the story of her son's death.

~ * ~

He was just seventeen, mowing the front lawn on a Saturday afternoon, goofing off in the process and let the lawn mower go on its own. It crossed onto the lawn next door and bumped into the neighbor's birdbath, breaking it. He went to the neighbor's house and told the wife he had accidentally broken the birdbath, and then went back to mowing the lawn. The husband came outside, screaming and yelling at the boy, his rage building with each word. He had a knife in his hand and stabbed that boy to death. The man was arrested, tried, and convicted of manslaughter and went to prison.

The man's family moved because they were so embarrassed, distraught, and I suppose, felt they just couldn't continue to look at Sister Pianoheart and her husband anymore. After several years, the man got out of prison and went back to his family.

One day, Sister Pianoheart, who could

still see a few yards in front of her at that time, took a walk. She said she didn't know where she was going but knew the Lord wanted her to go. She had grieved for her only son all those years, angry at the man who had killed him, and when she learned the man had been released from prison after a few short years, she was even angrier. But she obeyed the Lord Lord and took a walk.

When she had gotten a few blocks away from her home, she felt the Spirit of the Lord tell her to stop in
front of a particular home, but she didn't know why. She stood there for a few minutes and then the door to the house opened and out came the wife of the man who killed her son. The women just stared at one another, and then Sister Pianoheart asked if the woman's husband was there. The woman was quick to answer no, but about that time he walked out-side, along with his children, and other family members, who were all getting ready for a family outing.

The man stopped in his tracks. Sister Pianoheart stood where she was, praying si-lently that the Lord would lead her because she had no idea what to say, and wanted to run away. Then the man walked slowly to her, and foot in front of her, he took her hand and fell to the ground, crying and begging her forgiveness.

Sister Pianoheart began to cry as well, and wrapped her arms around him, and said, "I forgive you."

The man's wife then hugged both and told Sister Pianoheart that the man had not had a moment's peace since that day. He didn't sleep much, and when he did, he woke up shouting, having nightmares about the boy he killed. Right then and there, Sister Pianoheart asked the man if he knew Jesus. The man said no, he knew Jesus could never forgive him for what he had done. She told him if she could forgive him, certainly an all-knowing, loving God could. So, she prayed with him and he accepted the Lord as his Savior.

~ * ~

By the time she had finished that story, I was bawling. I knew my problem had been unforgiveness, and if Sister Pianoheart could forgive a man who murdered her only child, I could forgive the people who had hurt me.

It wasn't immediate. I had to work it out every day because, even though I prayed and gave my anger and unforgiveness over to God, that old devil knew it was an easy shot to take at me. So anytime it came up, I immediately prayed and rebuked the devil.

But it wasn't until the following summer at family camp that I really had the chance to exercise in the physical world that which I had claimed in the spiritual.

My dad's oldest brother's wife, my aunt Vivian, came to family camp. As soon as I saw her, my heart began to pound, and I felt all those old feelings of hatred, anger, hurt, and resentment begin to rise within me. I had to leave the tent and take a little walk to pray and get my emotions under control. After all, my aunt hadn't done those things but in my mind, she was his wife, and she hadn't protected me. I returned to the tent, sat through the meeting and when it was over, I caught her outside as she was leaving. I told her what Al had done to me, and she, of course, denied know. I wasn't as calm as I planned but I asked her to talk to her own daughters and granddaughters, because he had molested them too.

In fact, later on, I found out he had molested nearly all of my cousins, and only God knows how many others. By the time my aunt and I were finished, she and I both cried and hugged one another. Did she talk to her daughters or granddaughters? I don't know, but I do know that our meeting was healing for me.

As for the other uncle, my mother's brother Gerald, he died a few years ago from cancer brought on by Agent Orange exposure in Vietnam. I learned he had also molested my cousins on that side of the family and his own daughters, but my mother said he had accepted Jesus as his Savior before he died. Whether he did or not is between him and God. But I hope so.

~ Three ~

So how do we go about forgiveness? How do we forgive ourselves and others? What is the secret to letting go of all that anger and pain? Honestly, there is no secret. It's not easy and it takes effort, just like everything else in life. But there are things you can do that will help.

Everything we do begins with our thoughts. Whether we are going to do something, say something, or even cover our mouth when we cough, it all begins with a thought. The mind is the realm of all action, so you must guard what is in your mind.

So, to forgive would begin with *not* thinking about all those people and things that hurt you in the past. I realize that not thinking about something can be difficult because when you consciously try to not think about something, it's the very thing you think about.

Begin first with not talking about what it is that hurt you, or who it is that hurt you. Now, I'm not saying don't talk to a counselor, in fact, you may find it helpful to speak with a Christian counselor or pastor. What I'm saying is don't gossip about those past hurts.

How many times have you been in the doctor's office, or in line at the grocery store, and heard a conversation between people that really sounds like a who-can-out-do-who with the aches and pains competition?

"Oh, my arthritis has been so bad, I don't even know how I'm getting around today."

"I know what you mean, I've got arthritis and bunions on both feet. Try getting around like that!"

It almost becomes comical when you think about it. People gossip about the worst things imaginable, and then try to out-do one another and make things even worse. Never have I heard someone gossiping about being blessed,

or being saved or telling another what God has done for them.

James 3:6 "...*the tongue is a flame of fire. It is a whole world of wickedness, corrupting your entire body. It can set your whole life on fire, for it is set on fire by hell itself.*"

Wow, what a concept! If the tongue is a flame of fire, it gets kindled from somewhere—your mind. Your thoughts are what your mouth speaks, so learn to speak life and joy and hope instead of doom, dread, and death. Once you quit speaking those very things that hurt you, you will quit thinking about them too.

Matthew 12:34 *"...for out of the abundance of the heart, the mouth speaks."* What is in your heart? Get rid of the garbage of unforgiveness, bitterness, shame, and hatred, and fill it with the word of God and prayer. Then, when you speak, you will speak life. Anytime your mind begins to fill with thoughts of your hurtful past, rebuke the devil in the Name of Jesus and begin to praise God. Shout "Amen," and tell Jesus how much you love Him.

When you speak about unforgiveness for those things and people who hurt you so badly, you are speaking death into yourself and those around you. That is exactly what the devil wants you to do, but you can guard yourself from him, and live in the fullness of the joy of the Lord.

Ephesians 6:11-18 *"Put on all of God's armor so that you will be able to stand firm against all strategies of the devil. For we fight not against flesh and blood enemies, but against evil rulers and authorities of the unseen world against mighty powers in this dark world, and against evil spirits in the heavenly places... Stand your ground, putting on the belt of truth and the body armor of God's righteousness. For shoes, put on the peace that comes from the Good News so that you will be fully prepared. In addition to all of these, hold up the shield of faith to stop the fiery arrows of the devil. Put on salvation as your helmet, and take the sword of the Spirit, which is the Word of God. Pray in the spirit at all times and on every occasion."*

These verses are your answer to everything that may come up against you in your life. No matter what the devil throws at you, no matter how rough life has been, no matter how, or who, hurt you, use these verses to stand against wickedness, no matter where it comes from.

~ Four~

God is love. God loves you. God wants to have a relationship with you. The only thing that stands between God and you is *you*. When you let your past rule your present, you will never move forward. You cannot go with God and stay where you are at the same time. You have to make the effort, no matter how much it hurts, to let go of those things you have been lugging around behind you, in order to have a right relationship with God. Letting your past rule your life isn't living, it's wasting a good life.

I cannot emphasize enough just how important it is to let go of the past and move forward. We can all remember things and people who have hurt us. We can also choose to hang onto those things and wallow in self-pity or let them go and revel in the joy that comes from a freed heart. Nehemiah 8:10 *"...the joy of the Lord is your strength."*

Depending upon the Lord for your strength, for everything you need, is the only way you are going to get through life. Forgiving others is part of that dependence, while un-forgiveness is a wall that you put up between you and God.

Matthew 8:22 *"Jesus said to them, 'Follow me and let the dead bury their own dead.'"*

Living with the dead things of your past will literally kill you, both physically and spiritually. Hanging onto the past keeps you looking back instead of looking forward and upward to Christ. The past is called the past for a reason. It is done, over, and gone. We have to let go of that which drags us down and look at that which lifts us up.

The second book of Samuel tells us when King David's baby lay ill, David laid on his face praying that God would heal the child. When the baby died, David got up, cleaned himself up, put on clean clothes, and ate a meal. Since this went against how people mourned in those days, David's servants were astonished to see their king acting this way.

2 Samuel 12:23 *"But why should I fast when he is dead? Can I bring him back again? I will go to him one day, but he cannot return to me."*

David understood that while mourning for his son was appropriate, continuing to lie devastated, not eating, washing, or taking care of his duties as king, he would not accomplish anything. David was God's chosen, a man after God's own heart, from the time he was a young man, and in his lifetime, accomplished great things through the Lord. We are like that too. God has great plans for our lives, but if we continue to lie in mourning, God cannot use us for His Kingdom. Unforgiveness causes us to lie in the dead, rotting, stinking things of our past. We are wallowing among the corpses of our past and sleeping in the cemetery of those things that are already dead. We cannot change the past, but we can change how we look at it, and how it affects our future.

I spent many years wallowing in the de-caying pain of my past, and then my grandson, Drake, died and I mourned that child for years as well. In my mourning, I could not hear God, nor could I accomplish anything that He had planned for my life. Although I was not suicidal and would never take my own life, I did pray for God to take my life. I was over, done, una-ble to lift my head and continue forward. I could not imagine that my life would serve any purpose because my mourning had consumed me.

This is not what God wants from us. God wants to lift us up, not watch us bury ourselves in grief and pain of those things which we can not change. But I believe that this is one of the greatest tools the devil can and does use against us. If there is a loving, caring God, why did He let all of this happen to me?

1 Peter 5:8 "...Watch out for your great enemy, the devil. He prowls around like a roaring lion, looking for someone to devour."

The devil is very real, and he wants to take us to Hell with him. He looks for those who are weak, just like a lion on the plains of the Serengeti. While those big cats will attack larger animals if they have to, they prefer to go after the weak and injured. The devil is like that. He goes after the weak and injured.

The death of a loved one, the loss of a relationship, physical abuse, drugs, crime, no matter what may have happened in your life that has left you bitter and resentful, has also left you weak and vulnerable to the attacks of the devil. But you have power over the devil simply by speaking the name of Jesus. That is how powerful our Lord and Savior is. The minions of hell flee at the name of Jesus. Hallelujah!

King David wrote, *"...weeping may last through the night, but joy comes with the morning."* Psalm 30:5

Memorize that verse and use it ever

time you feel as if the past is sucking you in again. You have victory because, *"...For every child of God defeats this evil world, and we achieve this victory through our faith. And who can win this battle against the world? Only those who believe that Jesus is the Son of God."* 1 John 5:4-5

There is only one way to overcome the pains this world brings to us and that is through Jesus Christ. No, everything won't always be peachy. The bills will still come due every month, you will still get stressed over raising your kids, you and your spouse will still disagree at times, but you will overcome these things through Jesus Christ.

John 8:36 *"So if the Son set you free, you are truly free."*

Calling upon the name of Lord as soon as you begin to feel as if the world is dropping in on top of you, will bring everything in your world into line with the Word of God. The Lord wants you to be free, joyful and happy in life. As children of God, we have a hope that goes beyond this world. It doesn't matter what things look like to us when we watch the evening news or see the horrible things going on around us, Jesus is bigger than those things. He is bigger than our problems, He is bigger than our lives, and He is bigger than our past.

As children of God we can rejoice in the Lord and be happy no matter what is going on. No matter what wars we hear about, are involved in, or the state of our government and governments around the world, we are free from these things because what God has for us it greater than anything the devil can use against us.

~ Five ~

Romans 8:1-2 *"So now there is no condemnation to those who are in Christ Jesus.
And because you belong to Him, the power of
the life-giving Spirit has freed you from the
power of sin that leads to death."*

Romans 12:2 *"...let God transform you
into a new person by changing the way you
think. Then you will learn to know God's will
for you, which is good and pleasing and perfect."*

~ * ~

These two verses teach us that first,
when we accept Christ as our Savior, there is
no more condemnation by God. If God does not
condemn us for our pasts, why do we continue
to do so? What is so wonderful about our sinful
pasts that we want to continue to revel in
them? Why do we beat ourselves up over something that God has chosen to forgive and forget?

Secondly, when we accept Christ as our
Savior, we also have to change the way we
think. Once we change our thoughts, which is
in our minds, then God transforms our minds to

His way of thinking. How wonderful is that? We step out of the destructive thinking that weighs us down and causes us to condemn ourselves and our past actions, into the way God thinks, first about us, and then about others.

If we would only take the time to view ourselves the way God views us in Christ, we would see we are beautiful, precious, clean, children that He loves so much we can't even conceive that kind of love.

Even if we must continually repeat words like, "God loves me." Or "I am a beautiful child of God." Psalm 147:11 says that God "delights" in His children. Don't you delight in your children? When they do or say something so cute, don't you just want to scoop them up and hug them? That is how God sees us!

Ephesians 3:17-19 *"Then Christ will make his home in your hearts as you trust in him. Your roots will grow down into God's love and keep you strong. And may you have the power to understand, as all God's people should, how wide, how long, how high, and how deep his love is. May you experience the love of Christ, though it is too great to understand fully. Then you will be made complete with all the fullness of life and power that comes from God.*"

I cannot help but get excited reading those passages! Our "roots" will grow into God's love, so if our roots are with God's love, never can the devil uproot us unless we let him. God's love covers us in all ways, all areas of our lives, without expectation, in the same way we love our own
children without expectation. We are literally adopted into God's family when we ask Jesus into our hearts.

Galatians 4:5 *"God sent Him to buy freedom for us who were slaves to the law, so that He could adopt us as his very own children."*

Ephesians 1:3-5 *"...we are united with Christ. Even before He made the world, God loved us in Christ to be holy and without fault in his eyes. God decided in advance to adopt us into His family..."*

God loves each of us so much that He sent His only begotten Son to die a horrible death on the cross so that we can become sons and daughters, adopted into the family of God as heirs to the Kingdom just as Jesus is an heir. Yet, Jesus had to die on the cross, while all we have to do is ask for forgiveness, which is given freely.

When that single drop of blood at Calvary fell on us, we became children of God. None of us deserve that kind of love. We have all sinned and fallen short of the glory of God. (Romans 3:23) There is nothing more we can do to become a child of God. We can't work for it, we can't buy it, we can only fall before God Almighty and in sincerity, ask the Lord Jesus to forgive us. And He will.

Romans 10:9 *"If you confess with your mouth that Jesus is Lord and believe in your heart that God raised Him from the dead, you will be saved."*

Even so, we do not come without the baggage of our sinful lives. We have to be willing to hand that over to God as well. It may not come immediately but you have a Savior who will help you. Again, all you have to do is ask. Why would anyone want to carry around their grief, pain, and unforgiveness when the Lord says, *"...Come to me, all of you who are weary and carry heavy burdens, and I will give you rest."* Matthew 11:28

Don't you want that kind of rest and peace? Wouldn't it be nice to lay down all the things in your past that have haunted you, caused you to be stuck in a rut, unable to move forward? God offers us *"...peace that surpasses all understanding."* Philippians 4:7

My past is wretched. I cannot believe I lived wallowing in that filth for so many years, especially when the easiest thing I've ever done is follow Jesus. Being a drug addict was hard. Being a single mother was hard. Living on welfare was hard. Being a torn up molested child was hard. Not knowing who I was or where I was going was hard. Being a child of Almighty God is easy!

If anything I've said has resonated within you, and you are ready to rid yourself of all the condemnation, hatred, unforgiveness, doubt, bitterness, resentment, shame, fear, blame, disapproval, anger, humiliation, and everything else that is not of God, and put there by a devil who
hates God and you, then please pray the following prayer with me:

"Lord Jesus, I know I have fallen short of your glory. I know that my past has hindered my present and my future. I want you to live within my heart and guide my life. Take my past and get rid of it. Help me to live the life you have planned for me. In Jesus' Name. Amen."

~ Six~

This chapter is for you alone. It is designed to help you identify those areas in your life that keeps you from fulfilling your destiny in God's plan. There is no right, or wrong answers and you don't have to share your answers with anyone but Jesus.

Your Feelings

1. I cannot forgive _____ because _____.

2. Whenever I think of _____ I feel _____.

3. My father was _____ in my life.

4. My mother was _____ in my life.

5. Because of _____ my life has been _____ in the past.

6. The one thing I would like to let go of is
   _____.

7. Sometimes I feel like _____.

8. My feelings about God are _____.

9. My feelings about Jesus are _____.

10. I think "salvation" means _____.

I have written the above to give you something to think about. As you contemplate your answers, remember that feelings are as changeable as the weather. When I got up this morning, I felt "good" but right now I feel "tired."

We all have feelings, but we must learn to control them, and discern which are relevant to the situation. We live in a world of overreaction, pleasure, and self-centeredness. We can be angry without shouting, screaming, and throwing things. We can be sorrowful without wanting to commit suicide. Learning to control your emotions is one of the greatest things we do for ourselves, and for those around us.

This next part is to help you to search

for biblical truths in your time of need. Many of them are already in this book but for every need you have Jesus is the answer. The Bible is a detailed plan for our lives and how to live with others, believers, and non-believers alike.

1. To accept Jesus as my Savior, I must _____ and be _____ in the Name of Jesus. (Acts 2:38)

2. So, put to death the sinful, earthly, things lurking within you. Have nothing to do with, _____, _____, and _____. Don't be greedy, for a greedy person is an _____, worshipping things of this_____. (Colossians 3:5)

3. ...Jesus, whom God raised from the dead. He is the one who has rescued us from the_____. (1 Thessalonians 2:10)

4. He personally carried our sins in his _____ On the _____ so that we can be_____ to sin and live for what is right. (1 Peter 2:24)

5. I am writing to you who are_____
   children because your sins have been
   forgiven through _____.
   (1 John 2:12)

6. We know that God's _____ do not
   make a practice of _____, for God's Son
   holds them _____, and the
   _____ one cannot touch them.
   (1 John 5:18)

All the verses above have the same theme—our salvation is based on the person of Jesus Christ, and the power of God Almighty.

Reading the above verses, and the passages from the Bible, do you believe that Jesus Christ can and will change your life?

Bible study is a key ingredient to your life as a Christian. The following verses will help put into perspective your place as a child of God and how the forgiveness of Christ applies to you.

> Psalm 130:4
> Matthew 26:28
> Mark 1:4
> Acts 5:31
> Acts 13:38

Ephesians 1:7
Colossians 1:14

I hope you will read and re-read these verses in the Bible, until you understand just how much God loves you. Join a Bible-believing church, a Bible study, or group. Many churches have study groups for new Christians, for men, for women, for teens, new moms, single moms, single dads, or whatever your personal need might be.

I also hope you will contact me and let me know if this book helped you. I love hearing your praise reports.

dancingwithbear@gmail.com
www.dwbpublishing.com
www.facebook.com/AuthorMarieMcGaha

About the Author

Marie McGaha is an author, editor, and publisher at Dancing With Bear Publishing, which is named in memory of her late husband, J. "Bear" Marler.

She is a mother & Nana, and she and her husband, Nathan are both members of the Patriot Guard Riders. Marie is an ordained minister with Full Gospel Pentecostal Churches, Inc. They live happily in the mountains of Idaho.